OBSER

Pocketbook

By Roy Watson-Davis

Cartoons:
Phil Hailstone

Published by:

Teachers' Pocketbooks
Laurel House, Station Approach,
Alresford, Hampshire SO24 9JH, UK
Tel: +44 (0)1962 735573
Fax: +44 (0)1962 733637
E-mail: sales@teacherspocketbooks.co.uk
Website: www.teacherspocketbooks.co.uk

*Teachers' Pocketbooks is an imprint of
Management Pocketbooks Ltd.*

With thanks to Brin Best for his help in
launching the series.

This edition published 2009.

ISBN 978 1 906610 00 5

British Library Cataloguing-in-Publication
Data – A catalogue record for this book is
available from the British Library.

Design, typesetting and graphics by **efex Ltd**.
Printed in UK.

Contents

Foreword

In my seven years as an AST, one of the most pleasurable aspects of the job has been visiting colleagues' classrooms to watch them at work. I can think of no better way to spread good practice, offer advice, provide a united front against the best efforts of students to derail work, talk through ideas, model new approaches, offer a shoulder to cry on when things don't go as planned and give high fives and slaps on the back when lessons simply dazzle with brilliance.

I can also think of no other way in which I could have learned so much about how to teach, than by watching other teachers, taking away the ideas I have seen and implementing or adapting them in my own lessons. (OK, that's posh talk for stealing people's ideas!)

Foreword

Observation plays a fundamental role in improving the quality of teaching and learning. It is the most exciting and dynamic engine for whole school renewal and change, and it's a powerful way to inspire and motivate. Unfortunately, for many teachers – perhaps because in their schools it's only ever linked with performance review or inspection – observation is about as welcome as a poke in the eye with a sharp stick.

This Pocketbook is squarely positioned behind models of observation that support and develop teachers' professional practice. It is aimed at removing the negativity and stress sometimes associated with observation and at making it something teachers positively demand to take part in.

In the best schools
all teachers
observe other
teachers' lessons.

Why Conduct
Lesson
Observations?

 Supportive
Lesson
Observations

 Becoming an
Effective
Observer

 Observing
to Learn

 Inviting
Observation for
Professional
Development

 Effective
Feedback

 Personalising
Whole School
Observation

Why Conduct Lesson Observations?

Summative observation

The development of observation as a creative process has been a slow one, largely because of the way institutions have viewed the process. Until the 1990s, lesson observation was mainly confined to teacher training – the observer monitored, assessed and judged the trainee as part of the course. Once qualified, apart from a couple of observations during a probationary period, you could confidently shut your classroom door and build a world of your own.

Schools then adopted lesson observation as a management tool for recruitment and for checking up on teaching. It was writ large as the government inspection model, with external observers coming in to observe and grade lessons.

In some schools this model has been enshrined in in-house processes, which often use external criteria – typically, in England, Ofsted's – and employ the observer as 'judge'. It is a summative process and limited as a support for professional development.

Formative observation

In enlightened schools, observation is seen as a complex professional interaction. It's a creative, *formative process* personalised for each institution. Observation criteria are discussed and developed in-house. They reflect the best practice, views and vision of staff. Feedback is an integral part of the process. There are three types of observation in these schools. All take place within the same supportive context and all three are covered in this Pocketbook:

1. Observation for the purposes of **assessing** and **monitoring** performance.

2. Observation where the professional development and feedback are for the observer, not the teacher being observed. **The observer is the learner**.

3. Observation where the teacher being observed selects both the focus of the observation and the person best qualified to observe and support them. The observer acts as **coach** or **expert adviser** and the **teacher being observed is the learner**.

Observers as learners

Lesson observation has enormous potential when it is centred on teachers working together in a supportive environment to improve teaching and learning skills. It is a potent two- or three-way process that fosters creative professional development.

As an observer, you get to experience different styles of lesson delivery; different ways of setting up a classroom; a wide range of approaches to classroom management; and you get to see how colleagues of different personalities deliver lesson content (and sometimes the same content, but in wildly different ways).

As a result of observing and talking about what you have observed, you get to feed new ideas and approaches into your own teaching, to modify, broaden and sharpen your skills. You will come across not only new ideas, but also practical resources: worksheets, web links, starting tasks, even just different textbook pages that you can import into your own lessons.

The **observer as a learner** is a powerful driver for professional change.

Observers as coaches – everybody learns!

The observer as a coach or expert adviser is an equally powerful model.

And because observation is such an excellent way to transmit good ideas and practice, nine times out of ten the coach or adviser will pick up ideas from the lesson they are observing!

An NQT mentor/coach saw how one of the NQTs had developed a really effective marking technique: students were encouraged to write comments next to the NQT's own marking. The coach exported the idea wholesale into his own lessons, with very positive results.

So everybody can learn when they are part of the observation process.

Being observed

As an observed teacher, you can focus on aspects of your own classroom development. Being observed generates genuine and powerful self-reflection, makes you really think through how you are teaching and inspires you to raise your game. It also offers positive opportunities to discuss and consider a range of personal professional development issues, such as classroom management, teaching styles, lesson pace and structure, and learning outcomes.

For both the observer and observed, lesson observation is a dynamic tool for professional development. It encourages links between colleagues, improves the effectiveness of teaching and learning, and generates a positive atmosphere of mutual support and development.

The question is not why should lesson observation be undertaken, but why there isn't more of it in schools! The next two pages suggest a few possibilities.

What's in it for you?

Once you start looking at the opportunities lesson observation affords for professional development, the list is impressive:

- To demonstrate a skill
- To share a success
- To diagnose a problem
- To explore alternative ways of delivering a topic
- To assess performance
- To support a colleague
- To learn
- To coach
- To work out a solution to a problem
- To monitor progress
- To help with discipline

etc.

Observation scenarios

The example below sets out one school's different observation scenarios over the course of a term:

To demonstrate a skill: *an AST gave a lesson to introduce staff to a more effective way of starting a lesson.*

To diagnose a problem: *a student teacher who had particular difficulty with a group of Year 9 boys was observed to support her behaviour management.*

To assess teacher performance: *a number of observations were undertaken to allow a new head of faculty to assess his department.*

To learn: *a newly appointed, but experienced teacher watched a couple of Year 12 A/S level lessons to get a feel for an unfamiliar post-16 course.*

Have a go at compiling a chart for your own school or situation to see how many ways lesson observation could be used to support teaching and learning. The sections on 'observing to learn' and 'inviting observation' later in this book will help to broaden and develop your ideas, but first we're going to look at how to prepare for being observed for assessment and then at how to develop good observation skills.

Why Conduct
Lesson
Observations?

 Supportive
Lesson
Observations ◀

 Becoming an
Effective
Observer

 Observing
to Learn

 Inviting
Observation for
Professional
Development

 Effective
Feedback

 Personalising
Whole School
Observation

Supportive Lesson Observations

Protocols

This section looks at how to go about setting up supportive and useful observation when judging and assessing are significant elements of the process.

One of the most important steps is to establish a set of protocols. These add value to the observation process by:

- Allowing everyone involved to be clear about the part they are playing
- Setting out exactly what is expected in the observation process – and when
- Establishing consistency across similar types of observations
- Establishing consistency across subjects
- Providing a clear structure to follow to give focus to observations

Why do you need protocols?

Establishing protocols may require a degree of flexibility, but once refined to suit your professional needs they will underpin best practice. Keep them clear and easy to follow and make sure they achieve their objective of setting up a consistent, fair and helpful process.

The following pages suggest areas that need protocols and offer an example. However, it is important to personalise protocols for your school and your particular needs, so use the advice here as a basis for these (and see the final section of the book for further suggested frameworks).

One golden rule underpins all types of observation:

Share the observation criteria with everyone involved in the process.

Areas for protocols

There are two areas in which to create protocols: **preparation for observation** and **feedback**. They form the basis for effective observation.

1. **Preparation**. You need to establish: the observation focus; observation criteria; data to be collected and how it will be used; how feedback will be given. Eg:

- Will the teacher mark book be available, to give context to the observation?
- Will the observer sample student workbooks?
- Will the observer drop in and out, sample part of, or stay for the whole lesson?
- Exactly what criteria will be used?
- What written forms will be used?
- When will feedback be given?

There should be no surprises for the observee during the observation. Pre-arranged protocols will allow clarity and consistency when the observation is undertaken.

Feedback protocols

2. Feedback:
- What formal feedback will there be?
- When – and where – will feedback take place?
- What will happen to any notes taken during the lesson?
- Who gets copies of the feedback?
- How will any follow up of advice given take place?

The best protocols will be tailored to your own school circumstances, and will vary slightly depending on the type of observation taking place. Peer observations, for instance, will generally have fewer protocols than the more formal observations for assessment. But the basic principle is the same:

Good observation practice requires clear and supportive protocols.

The simple example on the next page could be used in most schools as a template for various observations.

'Drop-ins'

'A member of SMT will just be dropping in to see how things are going....'

'Drop-in observations' are often undertaken by senior teachers or middle managers to sample/get a sense of how a school or department is functioning. The following points provide a framework for good practice:

1. Focus of the drop-in is shared with all colleagues involved (ideally with an explanation as to why this focus has been chosen) two weeks in advance.
2. Observation criteria are given out – again two weeks in advance of the 'drop-in'.
3. Drop-in dates are shared with colleagues who are to be observed.
4. Agreement is made that written feedback will be provided for each observed colleague within a week of the observation.
5. Whole school/department feedback to be given as agenda item at next staff or team meeting. Staff will get a general overview of what was seen so they can reflect on findings. Individual feedback will, of course, be private.

With protocols in place for even a brief ten-minute drop-in, value is accorded to **everyone in the process** and the process itself will be fair and equitable.

Are you looking at me?

Preparing to be observed

For most teachers the prospect of being observed can be stressful. There are, though, a number of ways you can make the process positive and enjoyable. The following pages will help you as you prepare to be observed.

Let's get the bravest approach out of the way first! To get the most out of a supportive observation you could actually *just teach the way you always do*, making no extra adaptations or accommodations. It is tempting to put on a show, but resist teaching just to impress the observer; the best advice comes when you allow the observer to see you 'warts and all'. That way feedback is linked to your day-to-day teaching.

All the same, human nature being what it is and with self-preservation a high priority, a common approach is to teach a 'bells and whistles' lesson when an observer is in the room. The following pages provide a few 'bells and whistles' should you want them.

Pre-observation tasks

Before you are observed there are a number of things you can do to ensure your lesson shows you at your best:

1. You should know the lesson observation criteria in advance. Make sure your **lesson planning is sympathetic to the criteria**.

2. Seek out your **key school policies** on teaching and learning (best practice would see these reflected in the observation criteria). Make sure your teaching reflects the school ethos as laid out in the policies, eg if school policy highlights learning styles, plan in a range of activities to cater for them.

3. Be clear about what is expected of you in your planning – some schools expect observed lessons to be planned on a generic form; others don't require a formal plan at all. **Expectations will vary** dependent on the type of observation being undertaken: observation for assessment will generally be more formal than observation for development.

Pre-observation tasks

4. Demonstrate that you **have an overview of the class** and have identified students with special needs. Don't just plan for these students, highlight them in your mark book so the observer knows you are aware of them, and can see from your recorded marks the progress they are making.

5. **Show progress explicitly in your mark book** – a simple arrow system works well. After every 3 or 4 grades simply put an 'up arrow' ↑ for *progressing*, a 'horizontal arrow' ⟷ for *consolidating*, and a 'down arrow' ↓ to indicate *not developing*. Reading across shows individual progress; reading down reveals how the class is doing. Make sure the observer is given your mark book.

Use your mark book to demonstrate that you **assess** and **monitor progress**.

J. Smith	A B B	↓	B B B	⟷
A. Jones	C C C	⟷	C B C	↑
P. Brown	C D C	⟷	C C C	↑
M. Patel	B C B	⟷	B A A	↑

Pre-observation tasks

6. Give the observer some wider context to your lessons by providing a copy of the **scheme of work** you are following. If possible, give an outline of the next couple of lessons to show where you're heading. This can be useful in discussion as you can show how students develop skills from earlier lessons and will go on to learn new skills in future lessons.

7. Make sure you have to hand all relevant **student data** – for example copies of any **statements**, **external assessment results** and **target grades**. Ideally, the last two should be recorded in your mark book, but at least have the information available somewhere in your planning documentation.

Points 1-7, outlined here, show any observer that your lesson is grounded in a secure knowledge of the needs of your students within a whole class, whole cohort, and whole school context.

Ideas for a polished performance

For the observation itself, here are some examples of good practice that will help you:

1. **Make sure you have a punchy and well-paced first task**.
2. **Move around the room**. It is important to show that your teaching is inclusive. By moving around, all students can access you while you can overview their work and offer advice. Avoid being mired at the front of a room.
3. **Think about the kinds of questions you ask**, eg questions starting with 'What?' require a simpler response than questions starting with 'Why?' And be sure to spread the load – don't rely on just a few students to respond to Q+A sessions.
4. **Differentiate** – You need to *show* that you are differentiating. One way is to put key words/spellings on the board and then support students as you move around the room. Stand near to weaker students as you teach so you can support them quickly. You can demonstrate differentiation by putting simpler questions to less able students and by challenging more able students to summarise; for example give them only 50 words to complete a task.

Ideas for a polished performance

5. **Share the focus** of the lesson and the lesson objective with the students in a creative way. The simplest is 'Guess the objective': after each task ask your class if they can work out the lesson objective (which you reveal at the end of the lesson).

6. **Show progress** at the end of the lesson.
   - Ask class to list examples of what they have learned today
   - Ask students to contribute to a whole-class mind map of new ideas (see 7 below)
   - Ask class to give you one new fact each (or per group) as they get ready to leave the room

7. **Remember that mind-mapping on the board is your friend**. At some point in the lesson, pull student ideas together in a mind map on the board. This shows you monitoring understanding, reviewing progress, providing a revision point for ideas, as well as offering a change of focus/learning style.

A word about observation for assessment

It is fair to say that observations for assessment purposes are the ones that cause teachers most stress. It is also fair to say that they are the teaching equivalent of 'death and taxes': they cannot be avoided!

There are two models for situations where the observer acts as assessor/judge. In the first, whole school criteria are used to assess your teaching, and the observation is undertaken by a colleague. Ideally, there will be a formative element. This approach is dealt with in more detail in the final section.

In the second, an outside agency observes you teaching and uses a set of external (and often nationally applied) criteria for summative assessment.

Observation for assessment – knowledge is power!

In any observation for assessment purposes you will be 'judged'. This can be a daunting prospect, but if you are used to working as an observer and to being observed in supportive, formative contexts, observations for assessment will feel far less stressful.

It can be difficult for you to feel a positive part of this type of observation, but you can help yourself, as already outlined, by good preparation and by knowing and understanding the criteria against which you will be judged.

Most external criteria are available on the internet and it is worth taking the time to seek them out well in advance of the observation, so that you can plan accordingly. Also, try to get hold of examples of written feedback that other colleagues have received when observed against external criteria.

It may be a bit harsh to view this approach as 'know your enemy', but forewarned is definitely forearmed.

Case study one – NQT observation

A History NQT was formally assessed by her head of department using the national NQT criteria. The process was made as painless as possible by the head of department setting up a brief meeting a week beforehand with both the teacher and her NQT mentor. In this meeting the NQT criteria were shared and the precise lesson observation focus: 'dealing effectively with behaviour' was agreed.

In the following week the NQT and her mentor met to discuss the lesson the NQT had planned and to look at how well it would demonstrate her ability to meet the set criteria.

The lesson was then taught and observed. The NQT was given time to reflect and to apply the criteria to what had happened in the lesson. Debrief, focusing on how behaviour was managed, was then followed by a step-by-step review of the criteria and how the lesson matched them.

Case study two – don't be afraid to challenge

An experienced colleague was observed by an outside agency. Prior to observation he had printed off the published observation criteria from the internet. In the debrief, criticism was made of the teacher drinking tea while teaching. It was pointed out to the observer that the observation criteria didn't allow for such a judgement, and, furthermore, that the whole school policy was to allow intake of fluids in lessons.

By knowing the criteria, the teacher could challenge the criticism. The judgement was amended.

Becoming an Effective Observer

Getting started

Becoming an effective observer requires hard work. This section will help you build the necessary skills for supportive observation, whether you're in a coaching or assessing role.

You could be working in a peer trio, as a middle manager sampling how your department works, or as a senior teacher just 'dropping in'. Whichever, when you observe to support colleagues there are **two golden rules** to keep the observation process supportive, collaborative, and professionally developing:

1. **Discuss the precise focus** of the observation with the teacher, well in advance of the observation.
2. **Share the observation criteria** with the teacher, well in advance of the observation.

Part of a planned process

It is best to overview your teaching year and make observation part of a planned process.

Identify when in the school year observation can be most effectively used, and when it can best 'feed into' personal, departmental, and whole school planning. Some terms are much more intensive than others, with a heavier workload and various after-school commitments. If you want to create an atmosphere where lesson observation is supportive and positive, plan it in to less busy times of the year.

Seeing things clearly

Let's start with five things to bear in mind before you start observing a lesson:

(1) Think about how the room itself may affect the teaching

The room set-up may be out of the teacher's control, but it might affect teaching and learning quite considerably. Ideally, visit the room before the observation to take in its features.

One colleague had a regular problem with disruption at a particular table in one of her classes. Moving pupils had no effect. Attention at that table wandered whoever sat there. It wasn't until the lesson observer sat at that desk that the problem was solved. The table was in an acoustically poor zone of the room – in a corner and under a wall-mounted cupboard. As a result, the teacher was virtually inaudible.

A sympathetic observer will look to see if how a room is set up helps, or hinders, lesson delivery. Something as simple as whether the blinds work to let pupils see the whiteboard clearly can affect a lesson and may be outside the teacher's control.

Through a class, darkly

 Look at what is already set up in the room to support the lesson

Try to get a feel for the room. Is it full of stygian gloom or are there bright displays, perhaps of key words or assessment criteria, to support learning? Is there independent access to study aids – dictionaries, thesauruses, computers? Is there space for students to move around? Are there easy teacher routes around the room?

Does the room work as a learning space? In one room I visited, the whiteboard had been set up for easy access to the electrical points. So instead of being centrally positioned, it was 2/3rds of the way down the room. Classes had to cram into one half of the room to see the board and this affected classroom atmosphere.

Are the pupils sitting in rows/around tables/in a conference 'U'? As the lesson unfolds, has the teacher chosen an arrangement that supports or disrupts the tasks being undertaken?

You and your shadow

③ Where you sit and what you do will have an effect on the lesson

You will affect the lesson – it is unavoidable. So as you enter the room to observe, think of how your presence will alter the lesson.

Where you sit may well silence usually keen pupils, which may in turn lead to quiet consternation on the part of the teacher when lively discussion fails to materialise!

On the other side of the coin, your presence may curtail regular disruption. This can be easily recognised by the barely suppressed glee in the teacher's eyes as the lesson progresses smoothly (or you may notice a slightly desperate teacher 'busking' at the end of the lesson when content runs out because the planned-for disruption failed to materialise!).

You can mitigate your influence by moving to observe from three or four different points. This will also give you a better overall sense of how the lesson is going.

And finally...

④ **Know the observation focus(es)**

⑤ **Know the observation criteria**

And stick to them!

1. Look for outcomes to actions

Once the lesson is underway, there are some key ways to make your observation really effective. The first of these is to look for **outcomes to actions**. This will prevent your lesson write-up from being just a list of activities/tasks set, and will be more useful for feedback.

Examples:

> 'The teacher introduction was clear and **this led to** all pupils getting down to task.'

> 'The mind map gathered pupil ideas into one place and **led pupils to understand** the main points. It **also allowed the teacher** to monitor understanding…'

> 'There were simplified sheets for less able pupils. **This allowed** them to access the main lesson task…'

> 'The teacher moved around the room, **which allowed** her to contact each pupil and offer advice where needed. **As a result**, pupils made good progress with the task…'

2. Sample workbooks/student activities

By sampling books you will get an idea of how the lesson connects with previous work, and how marking and assessing is affecting planning. It will also allow more effective observation – beware the silent, well-behaved, but totally unproductive pupils! One colleague sat observing a lesson where behaviour was excellent, but when books were sampled, quite a few students had done virtually none of the tasks set.

It's a good idea to ask the observed teacher to let you know which students are particularly able, or which have special educational needs. As you look at workbooks and monitor pupils' responses, make sure you sample these students. This will give you a feel for student progress and allow useful advice to be fed back to the teacher.

3. Map the room – responses

Mapping is a helpful way of providing observation evidence that can be used to encourage good teacher development.

Example 1.
Draw a bird's-eye view of the room and plot students' oral responses to show how many pupils contribute (and who they are). It will reveal those who've been inadvertently overlooked, or over-relied on for responses.

The map opposite prompted discussion about how, in future, the teacher might include those students who did not respond. It also revealed that the majority of those who responded were boys and that most contributors were at the upper end of the ability range.

3. Map the room – responses

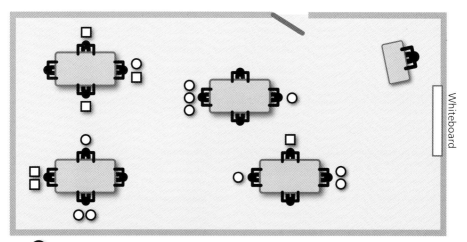

○ = Pupil responded to teacher prompting and answered question

□ = Pupil volunteered verbal response

4. Map the room – positioning

Another mapping activity is to log both where the teacher stands and areas of off-task behaviour among the students to see if there is a link between the two.

Example 2.
Draw a bird's-eye view of the room, and put a mark where the teacher is standing every 3 or 4 minutes. Also mark when the teacher moves to, or talks to, specific pupils. This will allow you to see how well a teacher covers a room, and how inclusive the lesson is. It will also help the teacher see if there are any areas of the room that they affect by avoidance.

You will generally find a strong correlation between misbehaviour and teacher proximity. In the example opposite, room coverage by the teacher is limited, and the less satisfactory student behaviour corresponds with parts of the room the teacher unknowingly ignores, or only occasionally references.

4. Map the room – positioning

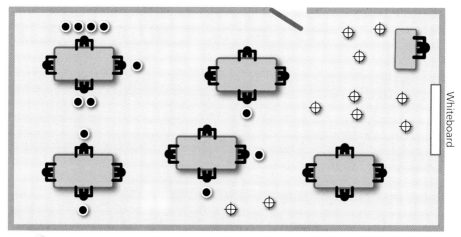

● = Pupil disciplined in some way

⊕ = Teacher location mapped every three minutes

5. Observe from more than one place

Try to get different perspectives on what is happening in the lesson by observing from more than one position.

We've already seen that this will help mitigate the effect your presence has on pupil behaviour; it will also allow you to see how the lesson looks and feels from other parts of the room. This can be very useful when combined with book sampling and behaviour watching, eg is there a harder-working or better-behaved section of the room? If so, you can use the debrief to explore why this might be.

6. Absence makes the art (of observing) grow stronger!

Leaving the room for a while will lessen any impact your presence may be having and will allow events to unfold more naturally. But also, observing is a very intense task, so leaving the room for a short time gives you a chance to refocus your concentration. This is a good time to have a look at the lesson plan, if you have been given one.

Do not be afraid of missing something vital; you can ask what happened while you were outside during feedback discussions.

7. Dance, trance or rock?

Consider what **rhythm and pace** there is to the lesson. One way to do this is to see if you can work out the planned structure without looking at any written version you may have been given. This is a useful approach because sometimes you will see a really good example of teaching that the teacher isn't explicitly aware of, which can make for positive feedback later.

If you have been furnished with a lesson plan, look at it *at the end of the lesson* and see how it fits with what you have worked out. If the teacher hasn't stuck to intentions, you can see how the changes relate to the original idea, maybe revealing, for instance, how the teacher has drawn on experience to vary or adapt tasks as they 'roll out' to make the lesson work better.

You should only ever use the teacher's lesson plan as a guide. Encourage flexibility – many teachers feel they have to stick rigidly to the plan handed to the observer. In pre-observation conversation make clear that this is not expected!

8. 'You can quote me on that...'
Log what the teacher says

It is often useful in feedback to discuss exactly what the teacher said in parts of the lesson, for instance when giving instructions and managing behaviour.

By writing verbatim what the teacher says when disciplining a student – and then linking this to how students respond – you can build up a clear picture of how well teacher interventions are working, and of how consistent the approach to discipline is. It may also highlight the odd unfortunate phrase that a teacher uses without realising that it causes problems.

9. Croak!

Voice coaching is rare in schools; yet good vocal skills are vital for a teacher. It's an often-overlooked area for professional development – sore throats and strain abound in the profession! Use observation to see how the teacher is coping with the vocal demands of the job. Consider **pitch and projection**.

Is the teacher projecting his voice? Voice projection is so important in a classroom, yet some colleagues talk into the whiteboard as they write on it, and expect students to hear what they say!

Is there any sign of straining? Does mumbling obscure explanation, or is discipline ruined by an inadvertently amusing pitch shift to ultrasonic?

10. Use your ears

Listening to classroom discussions can positively mislead you as an observer!
Don't be fooled by the apparent success of whole class question and answer sessions just because there is wide student participation.

Pay attention to *the type of questions asked*. Sometimes a teacher will get a false impression of how the lesson is going if the questions they ask are all simple 'describe' ones. Here is an example:

If you asked each pupil what was their favourite colour, you might notice everyone chipping-in quickly with a response. But if you asked, *'Why is it your favourite colour?'* some would struggle to answer as well as others. If you then asked, *'Why colour 'B' and not colour 'C'?'* the increased complexity of the question would pose difficulties for many more pupils.

To judge challenge and differentiation you need to use your ears carefully!

11. Be professional – respect confidentiality

Confidentiality is crucial to the observation process. Be careful not to allow pupils to see your observation notes. They are likely to spot any critical comments and could later use them against the teacher. If you leave your seat, *take your notes with you*. Likewise, students are adept at reading notes over your shoulder and also upside down! Look for a position where what you are writing cannot be read by others.

The same applies to body language. If you slump and look bored or dejected when observing, the students will pick up on this and react accordingly in later lessons. Make an effort to look alert and interested.

But beware enjoying a lesson! Sitting in rapt enjoyment means you are disengaging your observing brain – are all the students as engaged as you?

12. From 'x' to 'y'

As an observer you are looking for teacher impact and student progression. Listing what you see – the observing equivalent of a shopping list – does not demonstrate learning having taken place and doesn't help you to judge pupil progress, lesson pace or challenge. Always remind yourself when observing that:

Pupils entered knowing 'x'. (prior learning)

So,

Was 'x' developed or used? (reinforcement /development)

And,

Did pupils leave with 'y'? (new knowledge or skills)

Participant observation

There is one model of observation that asks the observer to take on an aspect of the teaching. Participant observation is best done once you are comfortable with the basic observation techniques already covered. It can be a powerful tool for professional development. Either the observer and the observed share aspects of the lesson delivery, or they swap roles during the lesson so that the observer becomes the observed and vice versa.

Example:

One colleague had planned the main body of the lesson but was interested in how to start it creatively. So the two teachers sat down together and the observer planned the opening minutes. When the lesson came around, the observer started the lesson off, their colleague making notes. Once the starter had concluded, the two teachers swapped roles.

This led to a very positive feedback session where not only were starter ideas shared, but also ways of adapting them for use as plenaries.

Participant observation

In another instance, in a school in 'special measures', the observer took on any necessary disciplinary intervention so that the teacher could concentrate purely on teaching.

This not only enabled the observed teacher to enjoy their teaching again, it allowed the observer to model effective discipline.

Ready to observe?

The previous pages have provided some ideas about how to take part in lesson observations, how to deepen the way you get a sense of what is happening in a lesson, and also how to avoid some common pitfalls!

Observation is a difficult skill and one that needs regular practice. You might want to approach senior colleagues to set up in-house training, using this book as a starting point.

The next two sections will look at two different types of observations – first with you in the role as a **learning observer**, and then as a **coaching or advising observer**. You will also learn how to use the opportunity of **being observed** to develop professionally.

Observing to Learn

The worker bee model

In the worker bee model *the observer is the learner*; so watching colleagues teach is part of the *observer's* professional development. It's called the worker bee approach because by moving around the school, seeing different subjects and different colleagues over the academic year, the observer takes away a wide range of ideas for their own teaching. They feed what they have seen into their own practice, and later into their department's practice.

The more worker bees a school has, the wider the cross pollination of ideas and good practice. The more varied the subjects observed, the better the professional development of the observer.

While you can set yourself up as a worker bee by approaching friendly colleagues on an informal basis, it is perhaps best to approach your line manager to build together a planned programme of observations.

Observing to learn

Finding the best match

Seeking out the best colleague can be difficult, so ask around to discover who could help. Your line manager might be able to recommend suitable colleagues. There may even be a school directory:

Example 1.

At one secondary school, all colleagues contribute to a sort of 'Yellow Pages', listing interests and talents drawn from their experiences outside school. This has facilitated some very powerful worker bee observations. For example, an NQT with extensive ICT experience outside of schools was able to develop some excellent interactive whiteboard lessons. More experienced colleagues, including senior managers, observed her teaching to acquire new skills for their own teaching.

Example 2.

Another colleague who transferred from a middle school was particularly skilled at teaching low ability, younger pupils. Various teachers watched his lessons to pick up ideas to feed into their own teaching. The observations stimulated positive discussions in department meetings about how to teach these students more effectively.

Looking for trouble

One classic worker bee observation is linked to behaviour management.

> **Example**
>
> In one school a subject-specific AST was used extensively to support cross-subject behaviour management. A range of teaching and non-teaching staff observed his lessons to see effective behaviour management in operation. Teachers were able to see how he managed the same difficult classes and pupils that they taught. Not only did this give ideas, it also underlined that some pupils were difficult to manage irrespective of the teacher. This helped experienced staff gain confidence that sometimes behaviour problems were not necessarily their fault.

In an extension of this, class teachers were also able to shadow individual pupils and whole classes, to see a range of behaviour techniques used by a number of different teachers in a variety of subject areas.

Think about how these approaches could support your own professional development.

Observation for training

Many schools use observation for training purposes, usually in a hierarchical way.

Examples

1. In one school, as part of their training and professional development, cover supervisors regularly observe experienced teachers. In other schools, beginning teachers and NQTs often observe established colleagues. And many schools include lesson observations as part of staff induction to help new recruits to get a feel for their new school.

2. In a similar vein, some heads of subject will model new lesson ideas for their team who then trial the material in their own classrooms. Showing observers how new content can be developed within their subject area is a very powerful way of managing curriculum change,

3. Many schools have observers watch lessons to learn how to observe!

Observation rooms and lessons on film

Some schools have purpose-built observation rooms where teachers can be watched to demonstrate good practice. Should your school have this facility, it would be good to plan a couple of visits into your worker bee schedule.

In other schools, lessons are sometimes filmed for staff training purposes.

These will not only help you to develop good practice, they will also allow you to practise your observation skills.

Paired observation

One very rich 'observation for learning' experience is when two people observe the same lesson (or part lesson). The paired observers select an experienced and skilled teacher to watch and then discuss what they see with each other, though the observed teacher might request feedback too.

Example 1.

Two colleagues observed a lesson with a focus on oral skills. They listed the various verbal activities they had noticed. One observer had a list of five strategies/actions; the second colleague had seven. In discussion the first observer learned some new ideas from the second observer, adding techniques they had not been aware of to their own repertoire.

Example 2.

A middle manager was paired with an AST experienced in lesson observation to help train the manager in how to make observation notes. Here the lesson was used to develop a technical skill in the observer. The middle manager was then able to observe her colleagues more effectively.

Peer observations – trios

Peer observations are an extremely positive and supportive way of spreading ideas and practice. In the peer trio model, three teachers work together to share practical ideas. The strengths of this approach are that friends work happily together, and the informal tone creates a relaxed atmosphere. Working in threes also alleviates any cover issues, especially if observations are done as short 'drop-ins.'

Example

Three teacher friends set up their trio. It was cross curricular – teachers of science, R.E. and music. They decided to focus on how to develop effective plenaries. Consequently, all that was required were short 15-minute observations at the end of lessons and these were all planned around times when one of the three had non-contact time. This meant that whoever was the non-teaching colleague could cover the observing teacher when he or she dropped into the third teacher's lesson. Once all three teachers had had the chance to observe, they then met to discuss the plenaries they'd seen. They went on to develop a bank of ideas to share among themselves and with their departments.

Peer trios in action

Observation played a key part when my school wanted to pilot a new 'thinking skills' programme. The trio who were asked to launch the pilot set up a cycle of observation and planning to see how the programme worked.

1. Trio met to plan lesson one.
2. One of trio taught lesson one, observed by the other two.
3. Trio met to plan lesson two based on observations of lesson one.
4. Another of the trio taught lesson two.
5. Trio met to plan lesson three in the light of observations.
6. Third colleague taught lesson three, observed as before.
7. Trio met to evaluate the run of lessons.

Each teacher *taught one lesson* in the programme, *and observed two* lessons. The observation schedule allowed the next teacher in the cycle – who had already had the benefit of observing – to review how the programme was going and to plan their own lesson more effectively.

This is a very useful model for introducing new courses or approaches: the observers become the engines that drive the teaching.

Why Conduct
Lesson
Observations?

 Supportive
Lesson
Observations

 Becoming an
Effective
Observer

 Observing
to Learn

 Inviting
Observation for
Professional
Development

 Effective
Feedback

 Personalising
Whole School
Observation

Inviting Observation for Professional Development

Come on in!

This section looks at a model of observation for professional development that is initiated and steered by the observed teacher. Here you **invite observation** to help you address a professional need. To get the most out of the process:

1. **Be clear about the focus you want for the observation**, eg teaching G+T students, starting a lesson effectively, behaviour management, in-lesson assessment. Try to avoid the 'just call in for a look' approach.

2. **Choose the right observer!** Having chosen the focus, decide who can best help you. You might already have someone in mind, but don't be afraid to go to your line manager or other staff for recommendations.

3. **Pick the right class to be observed**. Which class will give you the most opportunity for useful feedback? For instance, if the focus is behaviour management, choose your least well-behaved class.

4. **Select the best time to be observed**.

You may want to think about buying the observing teacher a small thank you gift for giving up their time to support your professional development.

Ask to be grilled but not fried!

A key point to remember is to ask for – and expect – questions and advice from the observing teacher that will require you to examine your own teaching. This can be quite demanding, especially as good advice will sometimes challenge your fundamental approaches and routines.

The following case studies will give you a sense of how observation for development works and some practical ideas.

Case study one – a matter of gender

A science teacher was concerned that he wasn't getting good work from the girls in his mixed ability Year 10 class. He asked an observer to focus on how the girls reacted in his lesson. The observer watched the lesson and collected data linked to this focus, specifically how the teacher interacted with the girls and how he asked questions.

In the feedback session, both teachers discussed the lesson and looked at the data collected. The observer then asked two questions, backed up with observation notes:

1. 'Why, when you asked the boys to contribute did you address them by name, but with the girls you just selected someone by pointing?'

2. 'Did you realise that of the 18 questions you asked pupils to respond to, 15 of the students you selected to answer were boys?'

Challenging questions that made for uncomfortable reflection for the teacher, but the point was taken and adjustments made. Both student work and classroom atmosphere improved.

Case study two – underachievement

An English teacher was concerned that a group of very able students in one of her classes was under-achieving. She asked for an observation to look at how that group interacted with her teaching. She noted in pre-observation discussion that their behaviour was very good.

During the observation, a discreet watch was kept on the identified group, the observer maintaining a very low profile. A selection of student workbooks was sampled and teacher position was mapped.

The feedback confirmed that the target group behaved very well, but the observer noticed that they only really worked when the teacher approached their table. This only happened twice in the lesson while other – less able – students received four or five teacher visits. As a result the spotlighted pupils were coasting.

The coaching advice was for the teacher to teach the next lesson as usual, but to watch how the group worked when she was away from them. The observation feedback was confirmed, and increased teacher presence near the targets' table saw their work improve.

Case study three – boisterous behaviour

An ICT teacher was having difficulty controlling a very boisterous class and asked for an observation focusing on behaviour management. After observation, two points came up during discussion:

1. *'Did you realise that when you helped a student at a computer you stood with your back to the class?'*

2. *'Why did you spend three quarters of the lesson at one end of the room?'*

Coaching advice included modelling a 3/4 stance so that the teacher opened himself out to oversee the whole class when giving one-to-one advice. Also, it was suggested that he move around the room more. On making these two small changes, lessons became more focused and orderly.

Ideas for observation focus

It can be quite daunting to decide exactly what you want an observer to look at to help your professional development. Here are some ideas:

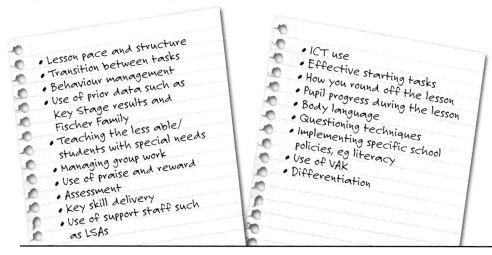

- Lesson pace and structure
- Transition between tasks
- Behaviour management
- Use of prior data such as Key Stage results and Fischer Family
- Teaching the less able/students with special needs
- Managing group work
- Use of praise and reward
- Assessment
- Key skill delivery
- Use of support staff such as LSAs

- ICT use
- Effective starting tasks
- How you round off the lesson
- Pupil progress during the lesson
- Body language
- Questioning techniques
- Implementing specific school policies, eg literacy
- Use of VAK
- Differentiation

A word about coaching

As an observer in this situation you will be acting as a coach. Coaching is a difficult skill and one that lies outside the remit of this book.* However, it is possible to look at two basic principles here:

1. A coach **teases out information** rather than telling. As coach, either ask questions or encourage your colleague to ask questions. If you have taught a lesson as a coach, the simplest approach is to ask: *'Why did I do that?'* Invite them to reflect and explain, before amplifying why you did what you did.

2. A coach **will listen more than they will speak**, again allowing the teacher to reflect on what they have seen rather than being told what they have seen.

The same principles apply if, in your coaching role, you have observed another teacher: *'Why did you do that?'* *'What were you aiming to achieve?'*

A good starting point is the Coaching & Reflecting Pocketbook by Hook, McPhail and Vass. Published by Teachers' Pocketbooks, 2006

Effective Feedback

What constitutes 'effective'?

Effective feedback underpins the success of any type of observation, be it for professional development or professional assessment. How feedback is delivered is crucial. Unsympathetic, insensitive or rushed feedback can mar the whole process.

Some aspects of feedback are common to all observation types:

- Agreed focus and criteria for observation leading to agreed focus for feedback
- A set time and place for feedback to be given
- Agreed format for advice, eg verbal or written
- Agreement over who has ownership of any notes etc made during the process
- Confidentiality

The following pages amplify these common aspects and also give examples of how approaches change in different situations. First, though, a word about setting targets.

Target setting

Setting targets is an important element of the observation and professional development cycle. Targets should be focused, relevant and have a clear review point built in.

It's a good idea to limit targets to two in number and reviewable within a fixed period of time such as half a term. This injects pace and momentum to the observation process and provides defined, achievable goals.

An effective framework for setting two targets is to choose one that encourages the teacher to **build existing skills** and another that encourages the teacher to **innovate** by adopting a new idea, piece of advice or approach.

Several of the case studies dotted throughout this book will give you ideas for effective targets.

Worker bee feedback

Feedback planning starts with an observation focus and you should start any feedback session with a recap of this.

In the worker bee model, you'll recall, the observer is the learner, and the observed teacher acts as a coach. Here, the teacher being observed needs to shape the feedback so that the worker bee can reflect and learn from what they have seen. The following numbered steps offer a real life example.

1. *An art teacher wanted to learn a wider range of behaviour management techniques for her difficult year 9 class. She sought out an AST who taught the same class in a different subject. After a chat in the staffroom, a clear focus for the observation was agreed.*

Feedback is sometimes hampered by the lack of a specific focus. In this case, the worker bee had a clear idea of what she wanted to observe to help develop her own skill. This immediately opened up useful and relevant feedback opportunities.

Worker bee feedback

Feedback needs to be given at a dedicated time and place.

Once the lesson had been observed, the two colleagues met after school, in the room where the lesson had been taught, to discuss findings.

> **2. The feedback started with the AST asking the worker bee to narrate anything she had seen in the lesson that was linked to behaviour management. Then she was asked to write a list of every example of behaviour management she had seen. This allowed the worker bee to reflect on the lesson both in conversation and writing. At this stage, the observed teacher takes a passive role. The aim is to get the worker bee to do all the talking. What did the 'observer as learner' see?**

It is easy (and tempting) to point out to the worker bee what they should have seen. But good coaching feedback starts with what the worker bee *actually* saw.

Worker bee feedback

Feedback values the skills a teacher already has.

> **3. The worker bee went through her list of what she had seen. For each example, the coaching AST asked the worker bee to rate how effective the behaviour management intervention had been, whether she had ever used that particular technique herself and, if so, how well it had worked.**

This opened up further, more detailed, reflection by the art teacher, not only about techniques she had seen, but also about techniques she had used. This let her see that she already had a good repertoire of behaviour management strategies, and the coaching conversation allowed the AST to offer one or two 'tweaks' to ideas she had already used.

For instance, both teachers used the technique of standing in silence to focus the class. However, the art teacher found that it didn't always work for her, whereas in the observed lesson it was always successful. The AST pointed out that he only ever used the technique after going to stand near the most troublesome students. The art teacher realised *she* had only used this method from the front of the room.

Worker bee feedback

Feedback introduces new ideas.

> **4. The AST then asked the art teacher how many different behaviour management techniques she had listed. She had counted six. The AST then showed her his list of ten different methods used during the lesson.**

This opened out a discussion, *led by the observed teacher*, of things that the worker bee had missed/not realised were behaviour management techniques. As a result, the worker bee was able to think about new techniques for her own teaching.

This approach allowed the 'observer as learner' to be led to new ideas, skills and approaches through the coach discussing his own teaching.

Worker bee feedback

Feedback encourages professional development.

> **5. Following the discussion of the new behaviour management techniques, the worker bee decided to add two of them to her own repertoire and to refine one technique she was already using. She also invited the AST to watch her implement them at some future date.**

If you look at the entire cycle from steps 1-5 you can see how effective the worker bee observation can be as professional development. It also builds confidence because sympathetic coaching, based on the worker bee discussing what they have seen and what skills they already have, is non-threatening. It is only near the end of the process, when new ideas are introduced, that the coach actually leads the discussion.

Top Tip: It is easier to move from narrative to analysis than from analysis to narrative.

A second worker bee example

In this example, an overseas science teacher unfamiliar with the concept of a plenary observed the last part of an experienced colleague's lesson. In feedback the scientist was asked to identify and describe the plenary task (a mind map summary generated by students writing on the board). The coaching teacher then asked, *'Why was that type of plenary used?'* and the observing teacher responded, *'Because it allowed students to sum up what they had learned'*. The coach pointed out that it also gave the students an active, collaborative task after twenty minutes of individual writing.

The discussion moved on to when the observer had used mind maps in his own lesson (he hadn't) and when students had been encouraged to write on the board (often). This allowed the scientist to reflect on his own practice and also to access a new idea, mind-mapping. This quickly became an observer-led discussion on how he could use mind maps to close his next lesson. It was agreed that after this had been trialled the two teachers would meet again to discuss how it had gone.

Here the observing teacher engaged in useful cross-department collaboration and picked up a new professional skill.

Feedback following observation by invitation

In this next situation, the teacher being observed is seeking feedback for the purpose of developing her own teaching, and has invited a carefully selected observer. In this case the observer is being encouraged to help the teacher reflect on her own classroom approaches.

There is a different feel to the most effective way to feed back. I call this 'the observer as questioner' technique.

Again look for the teacher to analyse their own narrative, but help them by providing your own narrative and by asking searching questions.

Case study – feedback following observation by invitation

One colleague had a particular problem with a class that would not settle. She invited me in to watch and for advice. The lesson was well planned and her narrative at the end showed a colleague who planned for a range of activities and learning styles.

In the feedback, I asked her to talk through her planning process, and then highlight parts of the lesson that went well. She had taken a great deal of time to plan a very diverse lesson with a number of well-resourced activities. It was clear that here was an outstanding teacher who readily gave time and passion to her subject, a fact I mentioned once we had talked through her lesson analysis. As for her difficulty in settling the class, I just asked:

'Why, if you were aiming at settling a noisy class, did you start with a whole class discussion that led to small group discussion?'

Sometimes you get too close to the planning and can't see the wood for the trees! In her next lessons, a simple structural change – discussion scheduled for later in the lesson – saw drastically improved behaviour at the start.

Feeding back after observing to assess

When you observe to make a judgement about quality of teaching – often using external criteria – it is important that you focus both your notes and your feedback on the precise criteria you are using, the point being that the observed teacher should know how they are doing compared with the model indicated in the criteria.

There is also the issue of fairness and consistency, given that observations for assessment are often done formally to evaluate the teaching and learning within a department, faculty or entire institution. As such, notes and feedback from each observation should follow identical paths, matching teaching precisely to each criterion.

Feeding back after observing to assess

Feedback should be very clear about why a teacher has successfully matched the observation criteria and/or *how they could develop so that they match the criteria in future.*

A successful way of feeding back in these situations is to start by asking the observed teacher to match their own lesson to the listed criteria.

It goes without saying that best practice would see the observation criteria shared with the teacher well in advance. It should also go without saying that excellent practice would involve the teacher contributing to the criteria in the first place.

Practice made perfect

Not all observation for assessment needs to be driven by the observer. One overseas-trained PE teacher asked to be observed using the QTS standards to support him in achieving qualified teacher status.

Before the lesson, the observer sat down with the PE teacher and they went through the external QTS standards together, identifying which ones would be applicable in the lesson observation.

Afterwards, the feedback centred firmly on how closely the teacher had met the required standards. This proved extremely useful preparation for when the external assessor arrived later that term to conduct the formal assessment. The teacher passed with flying colours.

'The Columbo Approach' –
ask useful questions!

The rest of this section suggests questions for stimulating useful feedback.

'Which parts of the lesson went well?'
This allows the teacher to reflect on the lesson without introducing judgemental phrases such as 'good', 'satisfactory', etc. A powerful word to use here is 'and'. It encourages the teacher to tease out more of what worked, eg:

'What went well?'
'The lesson started really calmly and the students got down to task.'
'And?'
There was good contribution to the Q+A session.'
'And?'
'The main written task was done really well.'

The idea is to minimise what you say, instead encouraging the teacher to pick out key successes. Occasionally, if a teacher is unconfident or feels under pressure, asking what went well can trigger a negative response. In these situations, ***'What were you pleased about in the lesson?'*** is a good alternative, allowing you to provide examples if the teacher is unable to. 'Pleased' is such a positive word to focus on in feedback.

Questions to stimulate useful feedback

'How well did the students fulfil the lesson objectives?'
This allows the teacher to reflect not just on the students, but also on how well the lesson activities matched the lesson objectives. It can lead to a wider discussion about the appropriateness of the objectives set, and how far the teaching enabled pupils to achieve them.

'How well did your lesson plan fit with the way the lesson actually went?'
This question leads to exploration of how effective the teacher's planning has been but also allows the teacher to demonstrate flexibility in adapting to the needs of the students as the lesson developed.

Questions to stimulate useful feedback

'What pace and challenge did you notice in the lesson?'
This is designed to get the observed teacher thinking about planning, delivery and structure. It is more positive than asking how well the lesson was planned?

'What would you look to improve/change next time you deliver this lesson?'
This is a positive way of asking a colleague to explore what didn't go so well. It is also an opportunity to offer alternative methods without appearing to judge the lesson.

'How happy are you with the lesson and why?'
Another good, supportive way of encouraging a teacher to reflect on their teaching.

Questions to stimulate useful feedback

'Which parts of the lesson would you use again and why?'
'Which parts of the lesson would you change for the future?'

These two questions allow the teacher to identify and talk through elements of good teaching and areas that need further consideration. They encourage the teacher to make suggestions for improving their own practice.

Whatever questions you use to prompt feedback discussions, your aim should always be for the observed teacher to do the majority of the talking and analysing.

Why Conduct Lesson Observations?

 Supportive Lesson Observations

 Becoming an Effective Observer

 Observing to Learn

 Inviting Observation for Professional Development

 Effective Feedback

 Personalising Whole School Observation

Personalising Whole School Observation

Personalising the observation process

The following section will be of particular interest to senior and middle managers. It is designed to help schools personalise and standardise their whole school processes for assessment observations.

One step in this is for your school to develop its own observation criteria. Judging individual teachers against external criteria is a far less useful development tool for the school and its teachers than using criteria that have been **generated in-house, specifically for your institution**. Some schools even present visiting external observers with their set of personalised whole school criteria and ask them to use these in their assessment, rather than relying on a 'one size fits all' approach.

Over the next few pages you will find out how to:
1. Personalise observation criteria.
2. Develop whole school observation forms.
3. Put in place a framework of good practice for recording and feeding back.
4. Implement changes through an effective 'pilot-review-implement' model.

Reflecting school aims and ethos

Before you start to personalise your school observation *processes* it is important to customise whole school observation *materials* for your own environment.

The aims are **consistency** of use, **clarity** of outcomes, and a clear reflection of **school aims and philosophy**.

To achieve these you need to identify key policies and practices that determine the shape of teaching in your own school. A useful starting point is to ask yourself:

'What makes a good teacher *in my school*?'

This should then be reflected in the observation criteria.

Personalising criteria

Use school aims and policies to underpin your whole-school observation criteria; for example if you wish to use a grading system of 'outstanding → unsatisfactory', first identify what makes an outstanding lesson *in your school* and use that as a criteria framework. So if a key policy is to use a range of teaching approaches to cater for a variety of learning styles, this should be reflected in your criteria:

An outstanding lesson will demonstrate…	A wide range of VAK use, with a number of tasks reflecting the individual learning styles.
A good lesson will demonstrate…	A range of VAK use, with a couple of tasks reflecting individual learning styles.
A satisfactory lesson will demonstrate…	Limited VAK use with one learning style predominating.
An unsatisfactory lesson will demonstrate…	Only one learning style catered for.

Personalising criteria

You can then build on this by looking at other key teaching and learning policies and referring to them in the criteria. For example, school policy may state, 'Class teacher should use praise to encourage learning'. So, adding to the example opposite:

An outstanding lesson will demonstrate…	A wide range of VAK use, with a number of tasks reflecting the individual learning styles. *There was wide use of praise to encourage learning.*
A good lesson will demonstrate…	A range of VAK use, with a couple of tasks reflecting individual learning styles. *There was use of praise to encourage learning.*

To keep the criteria sharply focused, concentrate on four or five key school policies. When taken as a whole, the criteria should reflect the 'flavour' of teaching expected in your school. Every school will be subtly (or not so subtly) different from every other, reflecting their individual philosophies, ethos, expectations and values.

Personalised whole school criteria help all teachers and departments within a school to assess how they fit into the whole school vision.

A whole school observation form

The next stage is to develop an observation form that will **standardise practice**. The aim is to create a form that will be used for all formal assessment observations across the school. It should:

- Act as a record of what has taken place throughout the observation process, from **focus** to **feedback** and **targets**
- Ensure that the process is clear and has focus
- Be flexible enough to be adapted for other types of observation, eg in peer observation or 'worker bee situations', the observer might be able to use just the front and back pages

Suggested format

One of the most straightforward, flexible and user-friendly formats is a four-side A4 booklet. A simple front page could look like this:

Observation Form

Name of Teacher: ....

Date: .... Class: .... Observer: ....

Observation Focus: ....

Notes made while observing

Centre pages – left page

The two middle pages could carry whole school personalised grading criteria, with space alongside for the formal write up.

Observation Form

Personalised whole school criteria

(1) Outstanding teaching will include a wide range of VAK use. School rewards will be consistently and widely applied and all students will demonstrate progress in their learning.

(2) Good teaching will include a range of VAK use. School rewards will be used with a small number of students and some students will demonstrate progress in their learning.

(3) Satisfactory learning will include a limited use of VAK. Use of school rewards will be limited and only a few students will show progress in their learning.

Centre pages – right page

The right hand page, for the formal write up of the notes made on page one, allows for a grade directly linked to the criteria, eg:

Formal written feedback

The lesson demonstrated some outstanding teaching, eg the starter included pictures and discussion, which engaged all learners. As a result students made good progress and this was evidenced in the plenary where each pupil was able to contribute one new example of work learned.

The lesson demonstrated some good practice in that the teacher circled the room and awarded praise stickers to a number of pupils.

N/a

Overall grade for lesson – (1)

Back page

The back page is for the last step in the process – feedback and targets.

Observation Form

Any matters arising following feedback

1. Although you moved around the room most of the time, you had a tendency to overlook the students nearest the door. Make sure you cover this area when you circle the room.

Developmental targets from observation

1. It may be useful to be more specific as to why a reward sticker is being given. At the moment a general, *'You are working well'* is used. Try to explain what exactly is being praised.
2. Share your outstanding starter activity at your next department meeting.

Class teacher signature

Observing teacher signature

A framework for feeding back

All schools are time-pressured, but be sure that your feedback process allows both the observer and observed time to reflect. (It is good practice for the observed teacher to bring reflective notes about the lesson to the feedback session.)

To facilitate this, state a definite time frame for the feedback, eg 'within five to ten days of the observation'.

Aim to allocate a designated 'feedback room' in your school – it is a professional courtesy and provides privacy.

Finally be clear about:

- The length of the feedback session
- What will happen to any notes
- How developmental issues/targets will be supported

Supporting development targets and school ethos

Ideally the observation process will be tied in to broader professional development opportunities, eg:

* By setting up links with the school INSET co-ordinator, if a whole-school need becomes apparent from a range of observations, it can be planned into future in-house training
* Likewise, if the staff development manager is aware of individual identified needs, placements on relevant external courses can be found or particular resources provided

Personalising the observation process in your school will lead to targeted and tailored staff development and training. Teaching and learning approaches will then reflect the core values and qualities of your school.

Involving students

The next step could be to involve students in the observation process. The general trend in recent years has been to increase 'student voice' over a range of issues. The key to appropriate and controlled student involvement in something as serious as lesson observation is **discipline**. Protocols and processes must be clear and well managed.

Used wisely, student-teacher observation can have a positive input to professional development. There are two absolutely fundamental rules:

1. Students should not be given an opportunity to comment negatively on a teacher's teaching ability.
2. Students undertaking observations must keep confidentiality.

Consult and pilot

There are certain steps to take to ensure that student observation is successful and non-threatening. The following advice will help you to set up a pilot project:

1. Consult staff over the issue long before you introduce the idea to students. It is worth remembering that pupils already watch and judge lessons daily – every time they attend a lesson! In that respect they have a good deal of experience. You could use this as a starting point with colleagues. Then set up a pilot project with staff who are happy and willing to be observed by students. This way, colleagues who support the process (and who may well have ideas to contribute as the programme develops) will carry the pilot.

2. Teachers involved in the pilot project need to meet to set out clear student protocols, eg about confidentiality and how to act when observing. Not only does this promote good practice, it also means that other staff will get to hear of the protocols and may well 'come on board' at a later date.

Consult and pilot

3. The pilot teachers then choose pupils they think would be suitable observers. By choosing students who are able to react maturely and responsibly, the success of the pilot will be further supported.

4. Teachers and students involved meet to discuss protocols and ideas. For the students this lends status to the seriousness of the task.

5. An observation week is set up and student observers are paired with a teacher observer from the pilot group.

6. After observation the pairs meet to discuss the lesson and then meet with the observed teacher to feed back.

Points 5 and 6 are also essential in mentoring students as they strive to find the right 'tone' for feedback.

Student observation forms

Here are a couple of simple examples of student observation forms. Remember, in all things pupils should be channelled into looking only at positives. It is not appropriate to encourage them to think critically of teachers.

Student Observation Form

Teacher Observed: ....

Date: .... Class: .... Time: ....

Which parts of the lesson did you enjoy watching?

Pick one of the things you enjoyed and explain why you enjoyed it

Student observation forms

Student Observation Form

Teacher/Subject: ....

Date: .... Class: .... Time: ....

Explain two activities you thought were good in the lesson

List three things students learned in the lesson

Choose one reason to praise the teacher in feedback (something you really liked/caught your attention/would like to have done yourself in a lesson)

Managing student involvement

Student participation in the observation process of your school can be an important and exciting element of student voice, but the process needs to be managed carefully. If you implement the above ideas, you will need to monitor and reflect at each stage of the pilot to make sure that it fulfils the requirements of your school.

The next stage would be for all those involved in the pilot to feed back to the whole staff about their experiences. This should then lead to a second, wider-ranging pilot as more staff volunteer to be part of the project.

In conclusion

I have always felt that for most of their careers too many teachers have viewed observation as a process enacted upon them. I hope this Pocketbook will be instrumental in helping *you* towards a sense of ownership of the process as a powerful and personalised tool for your own professional development.

I passionately believe that by making in-house observation processes more user-friendly and by encouraging regular, creative use of formative observation, teachers' confidence about having their lessons watched – whatever the context – increases. This has to be good for professional development, for disseminating best practice and, ultimately, for enriching the learning experiences of our students.

Enjoy!

About the author

Roy Watson-Davis

Roy started teaching in 1992 and has worked as an AST since 2001. His professional interests include staff training, coaching and mentoring as well as developing ideas for student voice. In the course of his AST work he has observed and fed back on over 300 hours of lessons across all subjects and grades of staff. This book arises largely out of those experiences. He is the author of the *Creative Teaching Pocketbook* and the *Form Tutor's Pocketbook*.

Acknowledgements

My thanks go to all the staff and students at Blackfen School, and to Matthew Brown. Hello to Simon and Ann and anyone out there in the DPAS. I find inspiration in many quarters, so thanks to the music of Led Zeppelin, Deep Purple and Townes Van Zandt; to Russell T Davies for the superb Dr Who; and my cats Buster and Mitch. Thanks also to Topes restaurant in Rochester; it was while I was eating my way though their menu that the chapters in this book took shape.

Dedication

For Dawn, with love

Order form

Your details

Name _____

Position _____

School _____

Address _____

_____

_____

Telephone _____

Fax _____

E-mail _____

VAT No. (EC only) _____

Your Order Ref _____

Please send me:

		No. copies
Lesson Observation	Pocketbook	☐
_____	Pocketbook	☐
_____	Pocketbook	☐
_____	Pocketbook	☐

Order by Post

Teachers' Pocketbooks
Laurel House, Station Approach
Alresford, Hants. SO24 9JH UK

Order by Phone, Fax or Internet
Telephone: +44 (0)1962 735573
Facsimile: +44 (0)1962 733637
E-mail: sales@teacherspocketbooks.co.uk
Web: www.teacherspocketbooks.co.uk

Customers in USA should contact:
2427 Bond Street, University Park, IL 60466
Tel: 866 620 6944   Facsimile: 708 534 7803
E-mail: mp.orders@ware-pak.com
Web: www.managementpocketbooks.com

Pocketbooks

Teachers' Titles:

Accelerated Learning
Anger & Conflict Management
Asperger Syndrome
Assessment & Learning
Behaviour Management
Challenging Behaviours
Coaching & Reflecting
CPD
Creative Teaching
Drama for Learning
Dyslexia
Emotional Literacy
Form Tutor's
Fundraising for Schools
Handwriting
Head of Department's
Inclusion
Jobs & Interviews
Learning to Learn
Lesson Observation
Managing Workload
Primary Headteacher's
Primary Teacher's
Promoting Your School
Pupil Mentoring
Secondary Teacher's
Stop Bullying
Teaching Assistant's
Teaching Thinking
Trips & Visits

Selected Management Titles:

Appraisals
Assertiveness
Career Transition
Coaching
Communicator's
Decision-making
Developing People
Discipline
Emotional Intelligence
Empowerment
Energy & Well-being
Icebreakers
Impact & Presence
Influencing
Interviewer's
Leadership
Learner's
Managing Budgets
Managing Change
Managing Difficult Participants
Managing Your Appraisal
Meetings
Mentoring
Motivation
Negotiator's
NLP
Openers & Closers
People Manager's
Performance Management
Personal Success
Positive Mental Attitude
Presentations
Problem Behaviour
Project Management
Resolving Conflict
Succeeding at Interviews
Self-managed Development
Stress
Talent Management
Teambuilding Activities
Teamworking
Thinker's
Time Management
Trainer's
Vocal Skills